If We Can, You Can.

How to change your life through the experiences of others

by

Jules Wyman

Jules Wyman
Positive Belief Limited
5-6 Kings Court
York
YO1 7LD

www.juleswyman.com

Limits of Liability and Disclaimer of Warranty

The author and publisher shall not be liable for your misuse of this
material. This book is strictly for informational and educational
purposes.

Warning – Disclaimer

The purpose of this book is to educate and inspire. The author and/or
publisher do not guarantee that anyone following these techniques,
suggestions, tips, ideas, or strategies will become successful. The
author and/or publisher shall have neither liability nor responsibility
to anyone with respect to any loss or damage caused, or alleged to be
caused, directly or indirectly, by the information contained in this
book.

Contents

Dedicated to my continued inspiration.

My Granddad.

Introduction

Won't you come into the garden?
I would like my roses to see you.

Richard Brinsley Sheridan

Have you ever looked at someone else and wondered *how do they do that*?

I'm not talking about the awe-inspiring stuff like watching an artist perform, a scientist discover or an athlete achieve a gold medal. I'm talking about the everyday stuff. Like watching someone get their point of view across in a meeting with ease and confidence, no matter who else is present. Marvelling at the friend who is comfortable in any social situation, they seem to breeze in and feel relaxed talking with anyone on any topic. Or maybe you have found yourself wondering how she (whoever she may be) can make decisions without consulting 15 friends, the family, the dog and checking the weekly horoscope!

That's how I spent a good portion of my life, more than 25 years in fact, watching other people, in awe of how they seemed to *do life* and wondering the very same thing, *how do they do that?* How were they living, being and doing everything with what seemed to me such grace and confidence?! I thought perhaps I missed that lesson at school or maybe they were born with or had it gifted in their upbringing. But instead of getting curious and asking them for help, I sulked and slipped on the *poor me* shoes and walked every day believing that I was the only one who didn't have confidence. I had lucked out somehow.

Years later when I had hit rock bottom I discovered books, courses, DVDs, and research that told a very different story. A whole new world opened up and I realised I wasn't alone. It wasn't just me that felt this way. I no longer had to keep on those *poor me* shoes, I could choose some more helpful ones that would make walking much faster, fun and easier!

It wasn't just me. And it's not just you!

There are ways of feeling better about yourself and life.

There are ways to build your confidence whether you grew up in a household that encouraged it or not. You can start to feel comfortable in your own skin without having to change the world! All of this is possible for you, it must be, because it was for me. Once I realised that this was possible, I became curious and began to look for solutions—just like you. That's why you've chosen this book…right? To look for solutions; a way of living differently.

About Me

Hi.

I'm Jules Wyman. I am the lead coach at Positive Belief Limited. I specialise in *confidence matters* and have coached and spoken on the topic for more than a decade. I love uncovering the myths and truths around confidence—self esteem, self belief, self worth etc. This quest has led me all over the world, having conversations across genders and cultures. Like Indiana Jones, I'm a seeker. I like to dig, looking for the root of the situation and discovering the deeper patterns of suffering and strategies, which manifest on the surface as various behaviours.

It may seem an obvious statement to make, but when you meet someone for the first time, you meet them as they are now, today. There may be some physical indications as to their life before—clothing, scars, or the way they move—but there are few clues on the surface that reveal that person's journey. Unless they choose to open up and share their story/past you only have insight into the present day person.

I hadn't realised this until I started a new chapter in my life. My working career had been spent around people who were aware of my story. They knew my background; my scars. But in 2003, I took a leap of faith and left that working environment. After a few years of exploring what to do next, and often floundering, I began running my own business, moving in different circles, and meeting new people that were unfamiliar with my journey.

When they met me they made assumptions that had always been like this. They assumed my education level and my upbringing. They saw a *confident, positive and inspiring business woman*, words reflected back to me time and time again. They found me to be just as comfortable talking to the teams at top law firms as I was delivering workshops in schools. By then I was, but it hadn't always been that way.

In the process of training as a coach I had managed to dispel many of the myths about confidence and so I no longer felt the need to share my story. Frankly, I was bored of hearing it! Who would be interested in hearing about me? After all, I wasn't anyone special. It was liberating to be able to put it all behind me and move on. Build on becoming the new person I had created. But the more people I met, the more I realised that sharing my story and my own journey of transformation from self doubt, negativity, and self hatred to an award winning business woman was important. Otherwise they assumed this was the way that I had always been and therefore life was bound to be *easy* for me. I wanted them to know the ladder I had climbed to be where I am, not because I am special but because it was a simple way of showing others that they can do the same. It may not happen overnight, it may not be easy but I want everyone to know that it is possible, no matter where you are starting from!

Since then I have shared my story in a variety of ways—speaking, videos, eBooks, interviews, radio, TV. My intention is to demonstrate that it is possible for someone to change. You can create a different way of living and, ultimately, create a different life.

If I can, they can. If I can, you can!

I would love to say that there is a quick fix and that this is it! But I value honesty and I know it is not always easy to make the changes that you want. You have to face aspects of yourself and life that you have spent years hiding from. Change is not an overnight occurrence. It has taken you years to get to where you are now so expecting to create new changes and perspectives immediately is irresponsible, impractical and illogical. Another way of looking at it is that you can't go from being a 5 year old to a 15 year old over night. Even if you did (and there are plenty of movies out there that play with this premise) you'd be a 5 year old in a 15 year old's body. You wouldn't have had all the training or experiences yet to be a 15 year old. It's the same with this kind of change. No matter how hard I worked and as much as I wanted it to happen overnight it didn't. I have grown into it, step-by-step, exercise-by-exercise and lesson-by-lesson. It may not be possible overnight but I assure you that it is possible!

When I share my stories of self-doubt and fear, I am asked one question repeatedly: HOW? How do you or how have you done it? My answer is simple, but it's not easy:

Every day I make a choice to put effort into my personal growth. If I am not learning, then I am not growing; and if I am not growing, then I am resting; and if I rest for too long, I will rust. I know the path that took me on before: one of self-destruction through overeating, drinking, smoking, and drugs. That is somewhere that I am not prepared to go back to, so I make different choices daily, consistently —and that's not easy!

For me, to put that effort into myself and to support my personal growth daily is a priority now. After all, I have to live with me for the rest of my life and I want that to be *happily ever after*. I want to be as loving, kind, and understanding as I possibly can, and after years of internal and external self-abuse that has been a challenge.

I am blessed to have people around me to support me, both personally and professionally. I have actively looked to be around supportive people and have worked with a number of coaches to keep me working through those challenges. I appreciate that this isn't the case for everyone, which is one of the reasons for writing this book.

About This Book

Some people have a moment in their life that they can see as the turning point. I didn't have one BIG THUNDERBOLT. Instead, it has been a series of storms. Some of the gales knocked me down, whilst with others, I didn't even feel the breeze. Some of the subtle disturbances took time to realise and sink in.

In part one of this book I will share three of these storms and how they made a significant impact on my life, either in the moment or upon later reflection. These stories are true and their lessons have been a powerful influence on my life.

Although I would love to find the elusive magic wand or secret weapon that helps others make big change in their lives, so that they can avoid the storms. There aren't any. And I speak from both personal experience and as a professional confidence coach.

In fact, when I am asked what the magic secret is to making change that lasts, my answer rarely satisfies.

Creating lasting change comes from patience and consistent effort—but how? That is a challenging question to answer as there are all sorts of solutions.

I discovered that what worked for me didn't always work for others. There are many different routes, as evidenced by the people I have been fortunate enough to work with.

Whilst I was sharing *my* shortcuts, my clients were sharing others. So, I thought, *Who better to answer that question of how to create lasting change than the people that have done it for themselves?*

In part two of this book, these lovely clients, ladies in this instance, will share their journey and their secrets to success. As you will read they come from a variety of backgrounds, ages and experiences.

Far too many people buy into a belief that you have to be special or privileged (financial, education, upbringing) in life to make changes, be happy and successful, whatever that may mean. Here, five *ordinary* women share their *extra-ordinary* journeys—all written in their own fair hands! None of them have climbed Mount Everest, but they have climbed their own personal mountains, faced their own sets of challenges, and have made significant, positive impacts in their lives and the lives of others.

Many people may be suffering from similar issues of feeling doubtful, fearful about what others think, not speaking up, worrying about sounding daft, or becoming overly concerned about how we look to others; however, each unique person has different ways to tackle these matters. These women have given you just that: a variety of tools, techniques, books, films, and quotes that have made a positive impact on their lives.

The final part of this book is the practical section. It's the place where you will find the tools, techniques, and a variety of materials to take the inspiration through into inspir-*action*!

All the exercises have been chosen by the women, and they are the *secrets* they feel have made the biggest differences to their lives, that they still use every day.

Read through them all. Notice which appeal and which ones don't. Choose maybe one or two at most and stick with these for a while. Notice whether they work for you or not. If not, pick another couple and practise those for a while. Again, test if they work or not. Keep doing this until you find the one(s) that fit for you and give you what you feel you need in any moment in time.

How to get the most out of the book

It would be easy to be flippant and just say *To get the most out of the book just read it and do the exercises!* I know it is more complicated than that.

There is a staggering statistic that less than 11% of the personal development/self-help books bought are read further than the first chapter. Only around 3% are read completely to the end and less than 1% of the information gets put into daily practice! Yet, people genuinely say they want to make changes and feel different.

To get the very most from this information, (or any information) you really do have to read it. All of it. Then make a choice. Do you want to stay as you are or do you want to do something different? Potentially very different. Do you want to do what is required in order for you to feel differently about yourself?

Once you have read through this book, make a choice as to which of the books, films, and exercises appeal to you and give them a go. Put them into practice. If you buy a book, read it! Read the whole thing, and DO the exercises. Having a top-class cookbook in your kitchen does not make you a top chef; you have to read it, put it into practice, make mistakes and learn from the process. Self-development is exactly the same! If you do not put the information/exercises into practice, make mistakes and learn from the process then nothing will change.

If you order one of the films, watch it and see how it relates to your life—and learn!

And, of course, when you do any of the exercises in this book, commit 100% to them! Turn off your emails and phone so that you will not be disturbed! Take the time to spend on yourself even if that is only 10 minutess a day.

Going to the gym once does not help you lose weight, nor be fit enough to run even a half marathon. To make these kind of physical changes you need to commit and be consistent. Do the exercises more than once—daily, if suggested, and for more than a week!

REMEMBER: it has taken you years of unconscious daily practice to be where you are now, how you are now. There is no magic wand/pill/guru that will turn things around *for* you, and it will not happen overnight. Be prepared for that. YOU have to put the effort in, and then YOU WILL receive the benefits. Be prepared for that too :-)

I appreciate that it may not be easy, and on some days, you might feel like you are pushing water uphill, but keep going. I have been working on this for more than a decade. It hasn't always been easy, but it is possible. You want to feel better about yourself and grow your confidence, do you not? Only putting in daily effort will support this kind of change.

So let's get started and read...

How I Did It

True Stories from Jules Wyman

Taking Off

When I was about 9 years old, my brother and I were invited by my grandparents to spend a day with them in London. This was a rare treat, so we jumped at the opportunity.

They took us to a large funfair on Blackheath Common. Before then, I had only experienced the small travelling fair that hit my hometown once a year and this was at least four times that size. I stood in awe, not knowing what to do. For my brother (who is two years older), this was *kid in a candy store* time—my Granddad felt the same too.

My Granddad is in his 90s now, and given half a chance (and if the doctors would allow), he would still be one of the first to jump on any fun fair rides—no matter what height, speed or spinning it involved. There was no stopping either of them. The moment they had finished on one ride, they were looking for the next adrenaline rush. I am not sure if it's a male thing or a family thing, but he and my brother were off in a flash to the Dodgems, the Big Wheel, the Wurlitzer, etc.

I stood and looked on, holding tight to my Nan with one hand and onto my candy-floss with the other. As I watched, I had that feeling inside. I suspect others have experienced it too. It's the one where you know that you want to do something, but you have that sense of uncertainty, not knowing how, or even if, you can do what it is that you want to do. Do you recognise that feeling too?

After a good while and plenty of screaming, my brother and Granddad rejoined us. They were talking at 100mph, recounting all the experiences and thrill of travelling at *those speeds*, what it feels like to be spun so much that *you have no idea which way is up,* and *oh the views from the top that are so high that you can see right across London.*

It all sounded like so much fun. As much as I wanted to experience it, I could still hear that niggling fear inside. All I could do was imagine what they were talking about.

My Nan and brother went off in search of food. More energy was required to keep up this pace!

You want to go on something? my Granddad asked.

Hummm... I looked up at him, not knowing what to say. I had never felt like this before. I had never faced the possibility of such excitement and yet felt so scared.

He knew.

This wise man looked at me with the kindest of smiles and said, *What if I could show you a way to do anything you wanted and never be scared. Would you be interested in knowing that secret?*

My eyes widened at the prospect of learning a new secret. Who wouldn't want to know a secret that could help you do anything you wanted and stop you from feeling scared? Right? Slowly, I nodded, mesmerised by his offer.

Together, like two great discoverers, we left my Nan and munching brother and headed off into the lights and noise.

First, he said, *look for a ride that you would like to go on—one that you feel a little nervous of and yet it appeals to you.*

I was attracted by so many, but with loud screams and noises, my attention quickly diverted. Finally, just as we rounded a kiosk, I saw them take flight. I am not sure if they still have them today but what I was looking at back then captured my curiosity and attention. They were shaped like small aeroplanes and could seat two passengers. They had small safety belts and in the middle of the two seats was a lever. These were planes that *you* could fly.

That's the one! I pointed.

Ok! he said. *Let's go!*

I was lifted into place, and Granddad took us through our safety check.

Belts on? Check. Smiles on? Check. Ready for fun? After each question, he would first check himself and look across to me.

Check! I beamed.

Now, all I want you to do is hold on tight and let's wait for it to start. Hold on, be ready with the lever, and, most of all, let's have some fun!

I listened to these golden words, and I was so lost in the magic and joy of the moment that I hadn't realised that we had very slowly started to move.

OK, are you ready? he asked

I'm scared, Granddad!

That's OK. It's just getting ready for takeoff. He had the warmest of smiles and soft chuckle. The ride had a sudden small jolt forward.

Now! he smiled. *Grab the lever now!*

I followed implicitly.

Now, you have control. You can take the controls now and go as high as you want. His laughter grew with his encouragement and reassurance. I took the lever and began to move it, smiling and laughing with him.

That's it, he chuckled. *That's it! Laugh as loud as you like, and go as high as you want. You know that you can always go higher or come back to where you want to be. It's your choice.*

Throughout the 2-minute ride, his repeated encouragement enabled our flight to move up and down, not always with grace and ease. At times, it was jerky and faltering, and every time that happened, he just laughed louder and smiled,

That's it! You're learning. You have the control. That's right.

He was of course right. I was learning. I do have control. His laughter and reassurance worked!

All too quickly, the ride came to an end.

Well? Granddad asked. *What did you think?*

I beamed and rattled out my 100mph appreciation of this special ride.

We skipped our way back to find my brother and Nan, recounting the dizzy heights of our maiden flight.

Tucked up tight in my grandparents' spare bed that night, I smiled and reflected on what I had achieved and at how brave I had been. Then, I remembered Granddad was going to share a secret with me. In the excitement of the flight, he forgotten to share it—or had he?

The Next Steps

When you're standing on a narrow path that even a mountain goat might think twice about, and very deliberately *not* looking down at the sheer drop below you because you have a fear of heights, the last word you want to hear from your guide is *goodbye.*

The man that had been helping me along the footpaths that twisted precariously up into the mountains of Peru simply turned his back and left me. Up until now, he had been doing a good job of keeping me moving along a trekking route that I would rather have chewed my right arm off than attempt alone.

"But you can't just... where? ...no!" I stammered in disbelief as I watched him disappear down the route I'd just nervously edged up. "**~?@!!!*"

I instinctively clung to the rock face for dear life, my knuckles turning white, my heart thumping blood in my ears, and my eyes stinging with tears. As I hung there, frozen in terror and more alone than I'd ever felt in my life, the all too familiar voice in my head began its onslaught.

Who did you think you were trying to do this?

You're no good at anything.

You were stupid to even try this in the first place.

So, how did a young woman with a crippling fear of heights end up glued to a rock face in Peru—with her nose buried in a rare species of lichen, her wrap-around sunglasses filling up with tears, and her heart sinking at the thought of never making it to the Lost City of the Incas - Machu Picchu?

Ever since I was a little girl, I'd always wanted to travel to Peru. Maybe watching too many episodes of Paddington Bear had engraved the destination somewhere on my subconscious, but I prefer to think some part of me knew that up there, on those treacherous paths, my life would change. Call it destiny; call it a soul calling; call it what you will. I just knew I had to go.

Somehow, though, I had reached 29 years old without ever getting near the country. At that time, my choices were controlled by the negative voices in my head. You know the ones. The "I can't" and the "what if" voices.

I can't go travelling by myself; I might get lost or hurt.

What if all my money gets stolen?

What if something really bad happened to me?

In 2001, I came across an advert for a trekking expedition to Peru in aid of Scope, the UK Cerebral Palsy charity. The trip would be a five-day, 100km hike through the Andean mountains, camping as a group, and supported by trained trekkers throughout the journey. It was the perfect solution for me. I could have my Peruvian adventure, travel with other people, and raise money for a worthwhile cause in the process.

A glossy photo of Machu Picchu was accompanied by the invitation:

"Would you like to discover the lost city of the Incas?"

"*Yes!*" screamed my heart. *"Yes, yes, yes!"*

"No! Don't be ridiculous," nagged my dominant negative voices. *"You can't raise that much money. You're not fit enough to walk that far. What if you fall and hurt yourself?"*

Thankfully, and uncharacteristically for that time in my life, I listened to my heart, and I booked myself on the trip in spite of massive fears and doubt.

I had just come out of a turbulent relationship, and whilst my new freedom was a relief, my self-esteem was still badly scarred. It took a massive amount of courage not to back out of the trip. The voices in my head told me I was a fool and destined to fail, whilst the voices of love around me supported and encouraged me every step of the way.

And so, in May 2002, I approached the 60 strangers waiting by the check-in desks at Heathrow. Nervous tears started to roll down my cheeks. What the hell had I been thinking? Lifting a pint glass had been the most strenuous exercise I'd done for the past few years, and here I was, about to fly over 6,000 miles in order to hike 100km through the Andes up to altitudes of 4,500m above sea level. "!!!!!"

As I headed for an airport breakfast, it felt like fear was kicking holes in my stomach, and the volume level of those internal voices increased to pneumatic levels.

What are you doing?

You can't do this; it's too much for you.

Turn back now while you can and go home where it's safe.

Don't do it you idiot. You're not fit enough. You'll die!

Through my blind panic, I could sense that there was a deeper importance to getting on that plane to follow the longing of that little girl inside of me who still dreamt of reaching Peru. I had no idea what it was but scared or not, I *had to go.*

Our first day in Cusco, Peru, was spent battling altitude sickness as we acclimatised to the thin air at 3,360m above sea level. Members of the group dropped one by one, with even the fittest retiring to bed in pain and nausea.

My worst battle, however, was still with the voices in my head. Our group briefing had tossed a whole new bunch of fears into the mix, and on the bus journey to our starting point, I was practically banging on the windows and yelling, "Let me off!" Luckily, my new friends encouraged me, and I found myself crossing a rickety little bridge with my fellow trekkers at the start of our adventure.

Within seconds, I was breathless. My rucksack felt like it was filled with rocks, and my entire body begged for me to stop. As more and more people overtook me, (included 60 year old Rita!) those internal voices were now screaming, "I can't do this!" I felt like a fraud. An absolute fool. I sat silently at lunchtime, worrying, believing, that everyone else thought the same of me too.

The pace slowed after lunch, and I somehow made it to the end of day one. The sun sank quickly, and we heaved our oxygen-starved bodies into our tents straight after dinner.

The next day, I felt a shred of confidence return. The sense of encouragement from the group was clear, and I felt boosted by a faint sense of optimism that maybe, just maybe, I could actually do this. My hopes were soon to be shattered.

After lunch, Helen, our Scope leader, briefed us on the afternoon trek, advising anyone with an issue with heights to stay back.

My stomach lurched. I had been so focused on my fitness levels and the fact that I was lagging behind and struggling to breathe, that I had forgotten that we would, at some point, be climbing up into the mountains—me, the girl who couldn't stand on a chair without panicking. We were crossing the Andes! All who had height issues were paired with a guide and luck, as it would seem, was on my side, as I was paired up with a Spanish doctor who would be holding my hand and guiding me through the trickiest parts of the trek.

Excellent! I thought. Not only did I have a personal guide, but he was one well-equipped to deal with medical emergencies.

And so, there we were, halfway across that insane mountain path with the rest of the group far out of sight, when some invisible beeper called him away.

Why he left isn't important; the fact that he left me was absolutely petrifying.

After several minutes of sobbing with fear, my eyes started to burn as they drowned in the salt water trapped in my tight wraparound sunglasses. My head was bounding from the screams and doubts inside, reminding me that I was *a fool to have even though I could do this. This was where I was going to die. I'm such and idiot.* I could hardly catch my breath.

I, tentatively, lifted my shades onto my head. And I heard a voice that was so distinctly different from the other judgmental screams, that I thought someone had come to rescue me.

"You can do this," it said quietly. *"Just take one step at a time."*

I slowly turned my head and saw an empty path. I was still alone.

"Just one step at a time," it repeated. *"Go on, Jules. You can do this. Just take it one step at a time; that's all you need to do, one step."*

The penny dropped, and I realised this was me—a positive part of me that actually liked me and wanted me to succeed.

"Come on, Jules. You can do it."

My heart started to do a little dance. I felt a surge of courage zip through my veins.

"You can do it!" exclaimed the new voice. *"Come on. You can do this."*

I gritted my teeth, took a deep breath, and shuffled my left foot along a few inches. I moved my left hand and quickly clung to a new part of the rock. Next came my right foot, tentatively sliding up to join its friend, followed by my right hand.

I did it!

I felt like a whole team of cheerleaders had exploded into a jumping, whirling, whooping dance inside of me.

"One more step!" shouted the voice with delight.

I made another slow side-step up the mountain—and another, and another. I kept going taking it just one step at a time until I had crossed the mountain, all by myself.

All the time, I had felt my heart singing as I realised what I was doing. Step by step, I was moving forward, moving away from the terrified, self-doubting girl frozen on the side of the mountain and becoming a woman who knew she could believe in herself and conquer her fears.

When I got to the other side, I collapsed—not from exhaustion, but from the sheer elation that I had actually achieved something by myself.

Now, I spend my life actively listening for and to that supportive voice, and whenever I face something that initially seems daunting, I think back to that path in Peru. I tell myself:

"You can do it. Just take it one step at a time."

Seeds Are Planted

Back in 2002, I spent a week at Findhorn in Scotland. It's a spiritual community on the northeast coast, where as a newbie you attend the "Experience Week" before heading onto any other course. The week is very aptly named, and I could spend the next few hours recounting the stories and experiences I encountered that week, but there is one event in particular which had a profound impact on me.

We spent the week on two sites: the hall and the park. We had lunch at whichever venue we were at. On the day in question, I was at the park. Ace! They created the most amazing and colourful lunches—all homemade and organic fresh produce. (My mouth is watering at the thought of it!)

As I queued eagerly for food, which hadn't even been brought out yet, I noticed a small man standing behind me. He was dressed in what looked like African tribal dress— not unusual to find traditional wear at Findhorn, the community attracted a global attendance. I half smiled at him and nodded. I was far more focused on food and the fear of missing out, than being polite and meeting someone new. A few minutes passed, and I felt the urge to look behind me again. His beaming grin was intriguing and had grown. I looked around to see who specifically he was looking at, and I realised that it was me. I politely said, "Hello."As I was about to turn back around, he replied, "Hi, Jules. Nice to meet you."

He stuck out his hand.

I hadn't met this man before or even noticed him during the week. I wasn't wearing a name tag, so how on Earth did he know who I was? As a spiritual community, Findhorn attracts all kinds of weird and wonderful people, including those who claim to be psychic. *Was he one of them? Could he read my thoughts? Did he know I just thought that?* Confusion and panic must have flooded my face as he reassuringly touched my arm and said, "It's okay. My wife is in your group and described you to me;

that's how I know you. She thought we needed to chat since we have both been to Peru."

Phew! A rush of calmness flooded my body. I could go back to thinking whatever I wanted safe in the knowledge that he wasn't reading my thoughts!

I now had the opportunity to talk about one of my favourite topics: my trip to Peru. I had been the year before and would happily "chew the hind leg off a donkey" with anyone to talk about it—whether they were interested or not! So, with one eye still focused on the serving hatch, we chatted about where in the country we had been and the magical sights of that fascinating place.

We both spotted the food arriving at the same time.

"It's been great meeting you, Jules. I am sure you would like to load up on lunch, so I will leave you to enjoy it and maybe see you later in the week," he said.

"Thanks. Been great to talk to you too." I replied and politely stuck out my hand. As his humble fingers wrapped around mine, he looked deep into my eyes. For a moment, we stood in silence. His smile fixed. Then, he asked a question that I had never been asked before and have never since: "How much do you believe in yourself?"

He'd caught me totally off guard. "Erm... I don't know... um..." I laughed, embarrassed at not knowing the right answer to the question. *Had we covered this on the course, and I hadn't listened? I'm going to look a right fool for getting this one wrong!*

"Seriously, Jules, how much do you believe in yourself?"

My laughter stopped.

"I don't know. I've not thought about it before."

I felt tense and uncomfortable inside. I had taught myself over the years to hide much of who I was. I even worked in an industry that allowed me to hide backstage. The actors I watched on a daily basis equipped me, inadvertently, with tools to disguise how I truly felt about myself. Now, I felt that this magical little man was looking past that and deep inside, and even if I didn't know or couldn't verbalise it, he knew the truth.

"Well, the usual amount, I suppose," I answered hastily. *What else could I say?*

Then, came the words that have echoed throughout each of my following years. With each year, they grow in strength and meaning. Still holding my hand and my gaze, he softly said:

"Believe in yourself. Your life depends on it."

He paused before repeating again, "Believe in yourself. Your life depends on it."

And again, "Believe in yourself. Your life depends on it."

27

The bustling dining room seemed empty and lost in time. We unlocked hands, but our eyes stayed hooked. It was like he was etching the words on my retina, engraving them deep in my mind to be revealed in depth and detail as and when I was ready.

I turned to rejoin the lunch queue, a question hit me, and I turned to ask him—but he was gone. I was lost in a momentary daze.

"Salad?"

"What? Er... sorry?"

"Would you like some salad?"

"Oh, er, yes, please."

Believe in yourself. Your life depends on it. It nestled deep inside—waiting.

It took around three years for me to even begin to understand the importance of those words. On their initial hearing, they were poetic, profound, beautiful, and even spiritual, but they were just words. I had knowledge of them, but no knowing.

Throughout the last few years though, I see new meaning each time I read them. Each time I speak them aloud, it is like another colour is being added. Like a great wine that has been left to mature, the depth, layers, and beauty of these eight words takes focus and understanding to appreciate.

Believe in yourself. Your life depends on it.

Wherever you are with yourself, believe, right now, that there is a new level that you can take it to—a new perspective that you can have.

Believing in yourself will take you to your next step. Whatever that may be!

Reflect, review, reuse...

Before reading on. I'd like to offer the space and reminder to pause. Take a deep breath in and then slowly, comfortably release it.

On reflection what did you gain from these stories?

Reviewing the insights, both the actual shared ones and your own personal ones, what can you take away from these stories?

Remember how great it is to recycle and reuse everyday, how can *you* use this information today?

There are no right answers to the questions above. You can only find the answers though asking the questions. Give yourself the space to digest, just like you would a great meal. Give your mind and body time to process and integrate the information, even if you are not totally sure what you are integrating. Just breathe.

And let's read…

How They Did It

True Stories from 5 Ordinary Women Living Extraordinary Lives—Written by Them!

<u>Claire (39)</u>

Life Motto – *"Being good enough is good enough!"*

Just over 5 years ago, someone asked me if I knew anyone who needed more confidence in their life. *Oh ha, ha! Was she kidding, or what?* Yes, of course, I needed more confidence in my life. At that time, whilst I looked successful on paper, and many people believed me to be very confident, I can assure you that I was not confident.

- My husband and I wanted to buy a house, but I was afraid of the responsibility and of making the wrong choice.

- We wanted to start a family, but again, I was worried that I would get that wrong and be a rubbish mum.

- I was a nail-biting traveller, who hated crowds, so I rarely went anywhere busy or abroad.

In short, I had confidence issues! When asked by a friend if I knew anyone who needed more confidence, I grabbed the leaflet and took the steps that changed my life.

During my first confidence workshop with Jules, I discovered that I spent a lot of time thinking about myself in ways that were defined by other people when I was a child. For example, I was miserable, grumpy, too sensitive, etc. I also felt that I "should" do certain things. I think I was living by other people's rules, rather than defining and living by my own.

My self-belief and self-image were very poor, and I just thought I wasn't good enough, or worth enough, to follow and achieve my dreams. My self-talk was negative, and I was very angry and frustrated with myself as I *knew* I could be so much better than that—I just didn't know how. I guess I got to the point when I realised that I had to make a change and either put-up or shut-up. Thankfully, I chose to learn new ways of "being" from various courses and coaches. I have most definitely improved my life in many ways, and I'm not finished yet!

I took the plunge and bought a house—something that previously I had felt too scared to do. It was in an area I didn't know, which was a big step out of my comfort zone. I became a momma to a truly awesome little boy and had the perfect birth! This was huge for me, as I didn't think I could be a good mum at all. My friends laugh at me now if I tell them this when they see me with my little man, but I really didn't think it was something that I could do. My image has now transformed from that nail-bitten, trouser suit wearing, scruffy at the weekend girl to a nail-polished, dress-wearing, high-heeled diva with fabulous hair and *loads* more body confidence. I saw some old colleagues a few weeks ago who didn't recognise me until I spoke! Oh, and I've started travelling and have been to some very large conferences too!

As well as these tangible things, I have become much more confident and comfortable in myself, and when new opportunities present themselves, I don't automatically think, *I can't do that;* instead, I think, *Okay, I can do this*! Or, I ask myself, *How can I do this?*

Yes, of course, I have days when I think I look less than attractive, that I feel useless or that I am rubbish; however, I know that I have strategies to get through these times and that they are not the true me. I also know that I am in control of my own thoughts and actions and that I can choose how to act, think, and feel. I guess I am just more aware of myself and what I need to do, or not do, to make my life as entertaining and joyous as possible.

The techniques and strategies that I have picked up during my journey that have made a difference to me are the following:

- *Visualisation*

  I visualised the perfect birth (everyday during my pregnancy), and I got it. I didn't just sit around day dreaming about it; as well as visualising how I wanted it to be, I also took the appropriate actions to make it happen. Everything about my little man's birth was perfect! Hmmm... I'm asking myself why I don't do more visualising— it's a brilliant tool!

- ### *Living with an Attitude of Gratitude*

  Keep a book of all the things that you have to be grateful for. We take so many amazing things for granted, and then fail to realise how blessed we are!

- ### *My Positive Notebook*

  In here, I keep quotes that I've gleaned from courses, lovely comments from other people, and a growing list of my qualities. When the going gets tough or I need a boost, I read my book (keep it in your handbag), and it really helps.

I think if you were to buy just one "self-help" book, I would get *You Can't Afford the Luxury of a Negative Thought* by John-Roger and Peter McWilliams. It is in easy-to-read chunks, and it offers every piece of advice and more that I've gleaned from lots of courses and other books.

As I say, there are "down" days, and that's why I think you have to keep in mind that this is a journey. Often, the destination, pit-stops, sights along the way, etc. keep changing, and that's okay. Make yourself keep it positive even though you may not feel like it, and remember: being good enough is good enough!

My goal in life is to be the best Claire that I can be, and I know that as a result of all the work I've done, I am much more amazing that I used to be. I also know that I've got way more amazing-ness to come!

Wishing you luck and happiness on your journey to amazing-ness!

Helen (25)

Life Motto - *"If you can dream it, then you can do it."*

If someone had said the above quote to me a year ago, I would not have believed them. "Yeah, right," I might have said, "dreams never come true." However, I know differently now, and that is why I have decided to share my story. It's been a bumpy ride, and I know I still have a way to go, but I hope sharing my story will help others to realise no matter how low they feel or bad their situation is that they can turn it around and make a change.

Writing this down is a challenge in and of itself for me, but I wouldn't do it if I didn't think it would help me and help other people.

From a very young age, I was sexually, physically, and verbally abused by family members. This made me feel stupid and worthless, and it actually resulted in me harming myself as well. I felt like I was trapped in this big, black hole, and there was no way out. I have seen and been through some horrific things, but it is now that I realise that this has made me stronger.

Until about a year ago, I was stuck in an abusive cycle, I had been living in my car, drinking heavily, took 2 overdoses, and was controlled by other people. However, as part of a "confidence" training course at work, I met Jules, and she gave me something no one else ever had: a compliment, a smile, her phone number, and, with that, a chance.

Over the past year, I have been working on myself with coaching, reading, and learning, and my life has changed dramatically. Using techniques such as *EFT* (Emotional Freedom Technique), I have learned ways to calm myself down and focus on the positive things in my life. I love doing *"splat boards,"* where I write down all the things that are worrying me, and then I talk about them. When I break them down, it makes them seem less scary. I also like my *"happy list,"* which is all the things that make me smile, so when I am feeling a bit negative, I can have a look.

I am not saying everything is completely fine, and I still have many moments of self doubt—but at least now I have strategies to deal with them. Even if I don't use these techniques, I am able to forgive myself and move on. No matter what your situation is, you can change it, but you have to be the one to do it. You have to believe that you are worth investing time in; because I can assure you, no one else can do it for you. People will help you along the way—Jules has helped me greatly—but ultimately, I have made the changes for myself. You can too, when you invest time and effort into yourself.

I like to think of myself now as a flower. I used to be a weed—no one looked after me, including myself, and I didn't live. I just survived. Last May, I made a choice to see myself as a sunflower seed, and I have worked hard to give myself water, sunshine, and hope. I am beginning to grow! You can, too. You just need to believe!

Good luck!

Wendy (41)

Life Motto - *"Stop looking for life and start living it."*

I lived in York, North Yorkshire, before migrating to Perth, Western Australia in January 2008. I am married, and I have 2 children. My son is 13, and my daughter is 11. I am an accountant and have been for over 20 years (!). I have always worked full-time. I was a partner in an accountancy practice in the UK. I am currently a manager in an accountancy practice in Perth, hoping to become a partner within the next 12 months.

I first met Jules for life coaching in early 2007. Prior to this, I had seen a counsellor, but I had found the sessions very depressing, concentrating on my past, when I wanted to focus on the future! What I needed was to equip myself with the tools to help me deal with all the issues which were currently going on in my life.

To recap to mid/late 2006:

I had good career, and everything in my life so far had gone "according to plan." I had subconsciously made a life plan up to the point I was at, and I was looking for the next thing... but I didn't know what this was. I needed new challenges and goals, and I felt things were getting a little mundane.

I then spotted an advert in the local newspaper for coaching, and I thought this will give me the future focus I am looking for. From the first session, I was able to start putting things into to practice. I even had "homework," which I loved!

In January 2007, I remember that it was a particularly miserable day, and I received an email at work from my husband, Harry. It said, "Hot, sunny, and 33 degrees in Melbourne!" He had heard a report from the Australian Open tennis tournament. When we were students, we had toyed with the idea of moving to Australia, but it never got off the ground. We then said we'd go for a holiday there when Harry turned 40, which was the following year.

However, that evening, we went onto the Internet and started looking into the possibility of migrating. We filled out a preliminary application and found out that we were eligible for a permanent residency visa.

My next coaching session was very interesting; the focus had turned from dealing with a big career decision to an even bigger, life-changing one! We had never been to Australia, and yet, here we were, making plans to give up our home and jobs to move to the other side of the world! This became the new goal! We had so much to tackle—all of which I thoroughly enjoyed putting into place. Harry was 100% behind the idea. However, we had to tell family and friends, and I had to deal with leaving my business partnership—all of which came with its own set of challenges. People kept saying, "You're so brave!" But I never felt scared, just very excited! We had so much to do!

I was amazed at how much of the preparation and plans for the big move just slotted into place. Two examples stand out in particular: selling our house and finding a job in Australia. We went to a number of emigration expos—one of which was across the road from where we lived in York, at the York Racecourse. It was here that I met what then became my new employer! I had been applying for jobs in Australia a few months previously—one of which was with an accountancy firm in Perth. I wasn't successful in getting the advertised job, but I recognised the firm at the expo. I went up and introduced myself. Long story short: 3 weeks later, in October 2007, I received a phone call from the firm offering me a job! The next day, we accepted an offer on our house. Some things are just meant to be!

It is amazing how much you can achieve when you find something that you are passionate about and are challenged by. The sense of achievement really does give you the confidence to "have a go" or try something new. The main driver for me was that I did not want to be sad, wondering a few years down the line... *what if?* Doing nothing was never an option!

The most challenging part of the journey for me was to be **patient** (not a strong point for me!), while we were waiting for the visa to be granted. Jules gave me ideas and inspiration to make the most of this time. As a family, we made a list of all the places we wanted to go to in the UK but had never been. Each weekend, we found a new place to visit—no matter where it took us. We had some memorable trips!

It was not all easy going, and there were plenty of tears and stress along the way! But my will to keep focused remained strong, and I would take a look at my *picture board* of Australia as my constant reminder of things to come. On December 19, 2007, with my mind firmly made up that our visas would be granted before Christmas, I decided to phone the Australian Embassy in London to see if they could give me an update. It was the best Christmas present ever: our visas were ready! I phoned Jules immediately!

We booked our flights just after Christmas, and we flew out three weeks later, touching down in Perth on January 23, 2008—just in time for Australia Day celebrations, which were amazing. Harry turned 40 five days later, so we did end up in Australia for his 40th after all!

Three and a half years on, I am still with the same employer, and my career has gone from strength to strength. My progression within the firm during this time has been immense, and my career has been given a breath of fresh air and a new lease on life! I have never enjoyed my job as much as I do now. I have been able to combine my accountancy skills with the life experiences that I have gained from migrating. I also took to the study books again, studying migration law, to become a registered migration agent.

Harry managed to secure a job within 6 weeks of arriving in Perth, and he also is still with the same employer. The children are thriving in school and settled into their new life admirably. We love our new lifestyle, and there is something to be said about the endless blue skies and sun—you just have to smile!

There have, of course, been some challenges along the way—not so much with the move, but events that I believe would have occurred regardless. Turning 40 was a big thing for me, and as a female, I am probably not alone in this! There have been phone coaching sessions with Jules since I have been in Australia, keeping me on track and focused and equipping me with new tools and techniques to "get me through life!"

One of the outcomes from our conversations was that I took up running two years ago, which is something I never envisaged myself doing. The results have been amazing—not only for my health but also for my state of mind! I now run regularly, and I am looking forward to taking part in the 12km City to Surf event in a few weeks' time.

When I sat down to write this, I realised there is so much I have done in the last few years; it was difficult to extract just a bit for you here. It has actually been a useful exercise to reflect, as there have been some considerable changes that have occurred to me personally. Life has been so full, and I hope it will continue to throw up new challenges and surprises!

And, if I am ever in doubt or have a wobble, I know who to contact!

Update: Wendy has just sent an email through to say that she has completed the City to Surf 12km run in 1 hour 10 minutes! And that she IS now partner at the firm.

<u>Sarah (27)</u>

Life Motto – *"Live well. Love much. Laugh often!"*

Who am I? Well, for starters that's a tricky question—even after 3 years of coaching! OK, I'm a 27-year-old primary school teacher from Wakefield—well, from the Northeast originally—living with my sister and the cat. Ooh! I'm also a trained life coach for young people, and I'm in the process of becoming self employed.

When I started coaching, I was negative about all areas of my life. I had just started teaching, and I didn't enjoy it. My social life was severely lacking, and I had zero confidence in just about everything I did. I found it hard to accept compliments and to compliment myself; loving myself was not an option and generally brought on feelings of guilt. My thought process was negative, as I felt I didn't have a right to be happy. In a word, I was a big VICTIM! The universe was very much a blur at this point! I was stuck in a rut, and I felt like I couldn't get out without a big crane—or, of course, Jules' "Chair of Transformation!"

It's been a long, but exciting journey, and I could go on and on for several pages! OK, my journey of self discovery began with a *list of qualities* (which I still carry around with me today). This list, made up of words from family, friends, and myself, set me on the path to self belief. Once I was on this path, many other tools helped me to keep going. Some of these are the *Golden Moments* book, encouraging me to look at the positives in my life, and *EFT* (Emotional Freedom Technique), which helped me to take control of situations that I had previously avoided. I learned to change my state and take control of the way I was feeling. This had a huge impact on my work as a teacher, since I started to enjoy what I was doing. Setting goals meant that I could achieve again and again, and then, of course, I had to celebrate these achievements no matter how big or small they were.

The *vision board* was useful when goal setting, and it allowed me to really consider what it was that I truly wanted to achieve. Having the board as a reminder encourages me to pursue these dreams.

I have referred to several books along the way including *The Secret* (which is fab), *Life Coaching for Dummies* (also brilliant), *The Artist's Way*, *The Self Esteem Bible*, *A Pocket Guide to Life Coaching*, and *Eat, Pray, Love*. I also found the films *Eat, Pray, Love* and *Yes Man* good for coaching insights!

I realise that before coaching I was living in my past, and for the future, now, I live in the present. The most important lesson I have learned during the coaching is that I have a choice. In the last 3 years, I have achieved more than I thought was possible. Bizarre as it may sound, my world is now very yellow with "Walking on Sunshine" playing in the background!

Yes, it's true to say that there are still days where I feel negative or slip into victim mentality, but I know how to change this and move on. I now feel empowered to set new goals, achieve more, and just enjoy myself! Since starting coaching, I have moved into a new house, trained as a life coach for young people, cycled Vietnam (well, not all, but a sizeable chunk!), and joined various social groups and clubs. I think the biggest change, however, is realising that it's OK to like myself—without feeling guilty or undeserving.

Fiona (50+)

Life mottos –
"It's never too late to be who you might have been!"
"Today is a gift; that's why they call it the present."
"If it's for you, it won't go past you."

I am a 50+ Commercial Director, and I have spent my adult life working hard to climb the corporate ladder in order to gain the respect of my family and friends and to be recognised as being "good at what I do."

A friend introduced me to Jules after I left my job, because I didn't fit in with the corporate culture of the organisation that I had joined, and I left feeling pretty battered and bruised. Leaving without a job to go to gave me the first opportunity in the last 30 years to stop—to actually stop and think about how I was feeling about life and literally take stock. It was a really frightening experience. I realized that I had been making sure I was always super-busy so that I could actively avoid doing this. It helped me to realize that I hadn't stopped to even think about whether I was happy or not; it had been far easier to just keep filling life with stuff to keep me busy so that I could avoid it. I couldn't go back, and I couldn't move forwards. I felt scared and "stuck."

Unconsciously, I wasn't even taking **responsibility** for myself and my actions. I would refer to myself as "you"— *You know, when this happens or you do that*—not "I" but "you." I also rationalized a lot of the decisions that I had made based on my upbringing and the people I had met along the way; so, again, I was unconsciously blaming other people and not taking *responsibility* for my choices. It was time to take *responsibility* for my life and my choices. My goal was to try and find some inner peace, rediscover the simple joy and pleasure in life, and to re-set my hope button.

I've been working with Jules for 12 months now, and when I think about how I feel today—which is so much more relaxed, happy, and peaceful—it dawns on me how far I have come. The road hasn't always been easy, and I hit a few potholes along the way. The worst patch was a few months ago when I did some serious wallowing, but this, in a funny kind of way, provided a valuable base from which to bounce back. The beauty of working with Jules is she ensures that, although I always feel really supported, the *responsibility* for moving forwards is mine. She doesn't give me any opportunity to abdicate *responsibility* for this, but she prompts in a way that is always kind and constructive.

I have also taken up a new sport—kayaking—which has provided some great metaphors for my journey over the past year.

- Life is about making small continuous corrections as I paddle along, which initially feels slightly awkward, because I am so conscious about making the corrections and actively thinking about it. However, with practice, it becomes more instinctive. These small continuous corrections help keep me on a path I feel good about. Even though I have a destination in mind, the real pleasure is in the paddling along, not on getting there as quickly as possible and missing half the pleasure of the journey—which is where I was 12 months ago.

• Sometimes I capsize, and occasionally, it comes as a complete shock. It's my biggest fear, and yet, when it does happen, it's surprisingly okay. Why worry about my biggest fears? I now know that even if it the worst does happen, I will cope. I will be fine, and in a funny kind of way, by coping, I will gain a renewed sense of achievement.

• I feel vulnerable on the water, and for me, being brave enough to not try and hide this has helped me realize that everyone, even the most skilled kayakers, feel this to some degree. By being open to this vulnerability, I have found that I connect with my fellow kayakers. The minute anyone needs help, the collective rallying to come to their aid feels fantastically protective and reassuring.

• When we play water polo, it's highly competitive and aggressive, and I love to be on the winning team. This does mean that I do get and give a few knocks, but I will always draw the line at fundamentally endangering my own or other people's safety. If it's unsafe or I could hurt someone else, then I draw a line—but not everyone else does. I accept that if winning is at any cost, then it's not worth it for me. I love playing hard, but if I have to play "dirty" to win, then I don't need to win that badly.

I now look at the world with fresh eyes—even down to how I think about a sport as simple as kayaking. I also have found that my appetite for self knowledge and understanding has made me want to read more. Again, this is where Jules has been fantastic in terms of recommending reading to help me on my journey. A couple of really enjoyable reads that I have found are:

- Susan Jeffers – *Feel the Fear and Do It Anyway*

- Richard Wiseman –*59 Seconds: Think a Little, Change a Lot*

- Wayne Dyer – *Change Your Thoughts*

My biggest realization over the last 12 months is quite simply that it's my life, my *responsibility*, my choices, so embrace it and accept the mistakes. Learn with good grace, and go forward with hope and positivity. It is no one else's job, right, or *responsibility* but mine.

About these ladies - 2015 update

Taking time to reflect enabled these ladies to acknowledge for themselves just how far they have come and the changes that they have made.

I still receive updates and I can honestly say that for all of them their biggest turning point was realising, as Fiona says *"It is no one else's job, right, or responsibility but mine to change my life"*. If it's not as you want it to be, you can do something about it. Maybe not immediately. They still hit bumps, potholes or detours, but they don't let these derail them. They have the tools that can make a difference, and they use them. Regularly.

So you've heard from me and the ladies, and, as I boldly state in the title of this book, 'If we can, you can'. So now, it's over to you again.

On reflection what did you gain from their stories?

Reviewing the insights, from the shared ones and your own personal reflections, what can you take away?

Remember how great it is to recycle and reuse everyday. How can *you* use this information today?

Remember too that it is just a process of learning; there are no right or wrong answers.

Now, let's discover…

How You Can Do It Too

Practical Ways for You to Make
a Difference in Your Life Today

Techniques for Getting Started

Now that you have read through all the stories, let's look at the practical application of some of the techniques mentioned so that you can make a choice as to which one(s) you want to use to create a difference in your life.

Have a good read through all of them, decide which one resonates with you, and give that a go. It is just as important to spot which of these techniques really doesn't appeal. Sometimes it is through doing that one that you gain your greatest lessons. What we resist persists, so its best to face it head on. Potentially, you will gain strength, knowledge, and even confidence in yourself, by doing the very thing you would rather not do!

Even though many of these exercises may appeal, make sure that at first you pick just one and commit to that. Yes, it does say start with just one. Once you have that under your belt, you can choose your next one or two. But to start with just choose one. There is no right one to start with, just go with your gut instinct, intuition, heart guidance or whatever way takes your fancy. Just make sure it's just one. Our minds have a habit of going into overdrive and wanting us to do 15 *new* things *every day,* changing it *all* at once! We are expecting or hoping that things will happen faster and change quicker. That's a bit like watering the plants with all the water they need for their whole growth in just one day. I am sure you can guess what would happen if you did that. It is not helpful to the 55 plant and it sure isn't helpful to you! So choose one of the exercises/techniques below, and commit to it for at least 7 days.

When your 7 days are up, take time to reflect. Many of the women have said in their stories that reflecting back has enabled them to realise just how far they have come. So make sure that you take the time to do that too. A great deal can change in just 7 days.

When you have reflected, no matter how far you have come, take time to celebrate it! You made a commitment to yourself and followed through, so acknowledge it in some way—take a day off, go for a walk, or treat yourself to a long soak in the bath. It doesn't matter what you choose to do and it doesn't have to cost any money. By taking this time, it helps your mind realise what you have done, and it becomes encouraged to do more.

Most importantly, be aware of self-judgment and criticism! This kind of behaviour will not inspire you. You will have days where you do not remember to do your exercise. That's normal, and everyone has them. Beating yourself up about it will not inspire you today or tomorrow, so be kind and give yourself a break!

Responsibility

I know that for Fiona understanding and implementing this has created a big shift in her life. It must have done as she has mentioned *responsibility* seven times in her story! It isn't an easy one as many of us have been brought up in a society where blame is nurtured or live and work in where blame is cultivated.

Most people who don't feel in control of their life are in **B.E.D**, and not in a fun way! They feel stuck and are not moving forward. These are the kind of people who BLAME—they blame others, themselves, circumstances, or even the weather for the way their life is, and that they are not where they want to be. What these people fail to realise is that by blaming, they are disempowering and de-motivating themselves!

Then, the EXCUSES come pouring out, sometimes disguised as reasons, justifications, etc. as to *why* things are the way they are and *why* they can't do anything more than they already have. Again, this is disempowering and is keeping them stuck, feeling frustrated or angry for not being where they want to be.

The final bedfellow is DEFENCE—not as easy to spot as its slumber companions, but equally as destructive. When someone is defending their corner they are not open to listening to what is going on and will potentially miss out on opportunities to learn and develop themselves.

If you really want to take control of your life, you need to listen out for this ménage à trois and stop the **B**lame, **E**xcuses, and **D**efence. Instead, collect the facts of the situation and ask yourself, *"Okay, if this is where I am now, where do I want to be?"*

Do you remember Wendy? She realised that she was wasn't where she wanted to be, so she took control to find out what she did want, made the plans, and took the actions to get her there!

Write your answers down—no matter how precise or vague. Take a break, come back, and have another read. Can you be even more specific? Where do you want to be? How do you want your life to be?

Now for stepping up and taking responsibility: How can you get there? You may not know the answer straight away, but it will come to you. When it does, take action. Get your life up, out of BED, and moving in the direction you want it to be!

Focus

There have been countless studies proving that your brain works on the guidance and direction you have given it. In much the same way as an Internet search engine works, you program in what you want it to look for, and it locates it. If that doesn't produce the result you were looking for, you change what you have put in the search box and keep going until you find what you are looking for. Your brain is like Google; whatever you are focused on is what it looks for.

If you put failure into Google, what results will you get?

Have a go. You can use any search engine. Put *failure* in as your search. What results do you find?

Or if you are more visual, hit images and notice what pictures come up.

Think about it: if you are programming failure into your **Google brain**, are you really going to feel motivated and inspired to take action? Does it mean that the opposite of failure—which I believe to be success—disappears? No! However, it does mean that you have to program in what you really want, and if that is success, then you need to search for it!

When you are not feeling at your best, ask yourself, *What am I focusing on? What do I need to focus on for me feel the way I want to feel? What do I need to programme into my search engine and actively search for?*

Wendy's story gives a great example of how this works. She knew something wasn't quite how she wanted it to be and was focusing on what was wrong, which is why she chose to see a counsellor. She realised that she was focusing on the past *"when I wanted to look into the future.*" Whatever you program into your Google brain is what it will look for!

As with many of these techniques, it isn't easy and takes practice and commitment, but it works wonders when you give it a go! So decide what exactly you want to focus on. If you are not sure if it is going to take you where you want to go, put it into Google; when you see the information that comes up, do you get excited or not? If it's the latter, then you need to change your focus!

Visualising

Visualising follows on from your focus as you need something to, well, focus on! I will use the true story that Claire has shared about her pregnancy. When she realised she was pregnant, her old fears reared their heads again—how she didn't want to give birth in a hospital, how she didn't want to take drugs, etc. Her focus had moved onto how she didn't want things to be: the negatives.

When she realised that, she stopped, took responsibility, and refocused. She thought about how she **wanted** things to be: to give birth naturally at home. Then, she used her imagination to visualise it all happening exactly as she wanted it to.

Our brains do not know the difference between imagination and reality, and so, you can use this to your advantage. When you imagine something to be real, your brain wants to bring everything into alignment to make sure this is true.

For example, Claire wanted a home birth, but didn't know if that was possible in her area. She visualised it all happening, and her brain went into overdrive. Looking for evidence, she found leaflets, information, and even overheard conversations that guided her towards finding all the practicalities she needed for this to happen. Spending the time visualising gave her brain the instructions to make this happen.

As she says, *"It's a brilliant tool!"*

Vision Board/Picture Board

To help your mind stay focused on what you want and the dreams you have, you can create a vision board; a picture board with your goals and dreams expressed in pictures and/or words.

Both Sarah and Wendy used this to stay focused on what they wanted to achieve. Wendy and her family/friends also created a picture board of all the places they wanted to visit before they left the UK. It was a great way for them to utilise their time before they headed off.

For Sarah, the vision board is a way for her to *"really consider what I truly want to achieve. Having the board as a reminder encourages me."*

A great way of doing this is to collect a bundle of magazines, and then set a timer for around 10-15 minutes. Go through the magazines quite fast, tearing out the images or headlines that grab your attention. The speedier you do this, the better—since you will tear out pictures you maybe wouldn't have thought about before.

Once you have done this, collect your images together and take the time to place them on your board. You can make as many of these as you wish or change them every few months/times a year. Make sure that you put it up somewhere where you can see every day. You can use this as your trigger for visualising too.

A quick true story. I had three inspirational men on my vision board, Tony Robbins, Jack Canfield, and Richard Branson. Next to them was a picture of a hotel that I wanted to visit, and next to that, a cross marked the seat that I wanted at an event. I had this on my board for a few months and looked at it daily. One day, out of the blue, I received an email with information about an event in a hotel that these three men were speaking at—together! Needless to say, I booked the event and went! And let's not forget Sarah who cycled across Vietnam and Wendy who now lives in her vision board—in Australia!

EFT

EFT (Emotional Freedom Techniques) has been mentioned by both Helen and Sarah. It has been impactful on their journeys, and it is a technique that they use for themselves too.

It is a simple yet remarkable healing system that reduces the stress that underlies much disease. It has proven successful in many scientific studies. It works on a variety of health issues, psychological problems, and performance issues, even those that have been resistant to other methods. It can be learned and applied rapidly, which has contributed to its popularity among millions of people. EFT Universe is the home of the vibrant, worldwide EFT community. It hosts the wealth of resources available to both experienced and new EFT users.

This is taken directly from http://www.eftuniverse.com/, and I recommend visiting here to find out more information.

I personally have found EFT to be effective on a number of issues for clients, from anxiety to blushing to stress. One of the reasons that I love to use it is because my clients can learn it in one sitting, and then, they can use it at home for themselves! If you choose to learn it or visit a practitioner in your area, if nothing else you will feel relaxed. Let's face it: if you're anxious about something, and then begin to relax, your whole day could change.

Positive Book

The amount of negative images and information that we are bombarded with is growing daily — the news, advertising, TV, radio, Internet, etc. You do need to make a conscious effort to look for the positives.

I realised this a few years back, and so, I began collecting quotes and pictures to put up around the house and office. I happened to mention this to Claire, and she now carries her *positive notebook* with her. It is a practice that I still do today and am now able to share directly with you.

Alternatively, look for the things that make you smile and collect them. Whether it's a sign in a shop...

...or it's an inspiring reminder on your pillow label...

...wherever you find positivity, make a note, take a picture, and collect that moment. Then, on those challenging days, you can look through your very own positive book and refocus your Google brain onto the positives of life!

Golden Moments

This is one of Sarah's favourite tools and I believe that she has used with her class at school too!

Golden moments came from realising that many of us have a default negative focus, especially at the end of the day. Many people mull over all the things that they haven't done, shouldn't have done, or variants on that theme. And so, they head off to bed feeling dejected and deflated from the day. Overwhelmed about the amount they have to achieve tomorrow, they toss and turn all night long, when all they want is to get a good night's sleep!

Change it. Go out and buy yourself a pen and nice notebook that you will enjoy writing in. At the end of the day, take 5 minutes to write down your golden moments—what you have achieved, what you enjoyed, when you received compliments, etc. Make it part of your bedtime routine. It's not about ignoring what has happened; it's about resetting the default. Sarah can now list the golden moments she has with ease. Those who do this as well find they also sleep like babies!

Splat Board

I have been using this for years, but it didn't have a name. Helen herself coined the name *Splat board*. It is a very simple yet profound exercise. It can support you from feeling overwhelmed with worry and stress to a place of calm practicality.

Think about a time when you had 101 things to get sorted and no time to get it done—and it's stressing you out. Everyone has had moments like this. The next time you feel this way, grab yourself a BIG piece of paper (I love using my flip chart for this) and a few coloured pens. Coloured pens are great at supporting your mind into thinking in a new ways and helping you move away from stress.

Using fewer than three words, write down the key areas that you are worried about—for example: finances, the kids, finding a job, passing my exams, moving house, getting married, etc.

Take a step back from the paper, and ask yourself, "What else am I worrying about?" When you hear the answer, "I can't think of anything else," you can stop. Then, look back at the paper and ask, "Okay, what is the *one* thing that is worrying me the most?" Once you have chosen that one thing, ask, "What can I do now, and what do I need to do next?" Write a list of the next steps that you need to take, and break it down into manageable pieces.

Go through each of the things that you are worried about, and look for the next step that you need to take or can take soon.

Like Helen, many people have found going through this process to be profound, as it puts life into perspective and enables you to realise what you can and can't do and, therefore, what you do and do not have to actually worry about. In fact, many find at the end of the exercise that worry levels have dropped and that there is a list of practicalities to get on with, one by one!

Asking for Help

In my experience, there are three things that are hard to say:

- "I love you" (and not expect the other person to say it back);

- "I'm sorry" (and not follow it up with excuses, reasons, or justifications); and

- "I need help."

The last has become a roadblock for so many because they feel that they have to do things themselves to prove their worth. Fiona mentioned this at the start of her story: "I have spent my adult life working hard to climb the corporate ladder in order to gain the respect of my family and friends and be recognised as being 'good at what I do.' It creates a need to control and have to do things your way, which stops you from asking for help!

By not asking for help, the doors of opportunity are closed to you, and you are in danger of feeding arrogance. Arrogance is not confidence! Arrogance is the son of insecurity.

By asking for help, all of these women made great changes in their lives, and rather than make them look weak for asking for help, it has given them confidence and courage to do even more than they originally thought possible!

Where and how can you safely ask for help today?

Patience

> *"There's magic in patience."*
> Brendon Burchard

Earlier this year, I heard this quote, and after all the other quotes, comments, and teachings I had learned about waiting, having faith, and being patient, it made sense. For me, it was the final piece of the puzzle.

It's very easy when we see someone *up there in the spotlight* to forget about all the work that they have put in to get where they are. There really is no such thing as an overnight success! As Tony Robbins says, "People are rewarded in public for the work they do in private."

We don't see the years of practice an athlete puts in to be picked for the Olympic team, nor the hours of practice and rehearsals that go into any ballet performance. How many times does a writer write, edit, and re-write again before they possibly get published? You see, most people focus on the end product, and they long to be where others are.

Many people are lazy. Yep I know it sounds like a harsh thing to say, but many want other people to do things for them. It's partly to do with how the brain works. It's looking for short cuts to save time and be efficient. Unfortunately for many this behaviour cascades into daily life as we look for the quick wins, shortcuts, and easy ways of doing things. Magic wands, a silver bullet or the special pill. Athletes may use drugs to enhance and improve their performance, but it can cost them their careers and their lives. Performers who don't rehearse are left behind by their peers, and so many books go unpublished every year because writers look for the accolades again without putting in the work!

It is the same with your life—no matter what you want to do or how you want it to be. Wendy and her family didn't just happen to end up in Australia, and as much as patience was "not a strong point for (her)," it was a major factor in the 12 months it took from making the decision to landing in Oz.

One of my clients made the wise comment recently that it takes daily effort to see yourself in a different perspective. Yep! She then followed that on with saying, "That's hard." My common retort, which I've heard said to me so many times over the years from so many great teachers, is this: "It's simple, but it's not easy!" Whatever it is that you want to achieve or change takes focused effort, each and every time you remember. This takes patience.

There is magic in patience, because when you keep putting the focused effort in and remain patient for the outcome, one day the magic will show!

Fear

Fear, or rather the illusion of fear, is the thing that stops many people from making the changes that they want to in their lives. Many of the above stories allude to the FEAR that has impacted lives, whether it is me at the fair in Peru, Claire being a mum and owning a house, Helen moving away from her abusive life, Wendy taking herself and family across the other side of the world to live, Sarah starting up new ventures, or Fiona taking responsibility and asking for help. What we believe to be real fear can get in the way and keep us stuck where we are.

The only real fear is a genuine threat to your life (i.e. if someone pulls a gun). People are wired for survival, and so when this kind of situation occurs (which is very rare!), fear kicks in to protect and do what it can to save them. That means that any other fear that you have is imagined, created, constructed by your mind—therefore, it's not real!

That's easy to say, and yet challenging, especially when you're in it.

Pull Back the Curtain

Have you ever seen the film *The Wizard of Oz*? There is a scene in the film when the wizard—"the great and powerful Oz"—is revealed as a little man behind a curtain with smoke machines, lights, and a microphone (to watch go to www.bit.ly/paynoattention)! This great, powerful wizard was constructed—in just the same way as the majority of your fears are.

When you realise that fear is stopping you from doing something, ask yourself, "Is my life in danger—really?" I imagine the answer will be no. In that case, just remind yourself that your mind is constructing this fear. "This fear is being created by my mind, and I can choose at any time to construct something more helpful."

You'll notice that the moment the curtain is pulled back to reveal the constructed *wizard,* he loses power. The moment you reveal the truth behind your curtain—that your fear has been constructed—it too will begin to lose power!

Qualities List

One of the first questions I asked Sarah was, "Can you tell me ten of your qualities?" I wish I had taken a photo of her reaction! It's not easy for people to see the qualities that they genuinely have, and yet, it's so easy to focus on what you believe you don't have or can't do. This tends to support you only in feeling down about yourself. So, one of the exercises that I have used both for individuals and in group settings is for people to create their *qualities list*—a list of the great things about that person.

The dirty looks and glares I receive when I initially ask people to write down their own qualities is hilarious, and yet when I ask them to tell me 5 qualities of a family member, friend or work colleague, they come tripping off their tongues.

I am not going to write much more here about creating your qualities list as you can watch the video here www.bit.ly/confidentliving, but before you click through, grab a piece of paper and pen so that you are ready to get writing!

Happy List

Every one of us has a cast of thousands inside,
including two of the seven dwarves: Grumpy and Happy.

The challenge is that when Grumpy comes along, he doesn't remember that Happy even existed! He needs to be reminded. One of the most effective ways that Helen and other clients found is to list the things that when they think about them, do them, or even just focus on them, create happiness. Some of these things could be the following:

• Spending time with family

• Walking on the beach

• A long drive

- A meal with a friend

- Spending time in nature

- Dancing to your favourite tunes

- Singing to your favourite tunes

- Curling up and reading a good book

When you have Happy in residence, grab your pen and paper and create your list. Draw it, photograph it, or record it in the way that suits you best, and then, when Grumpy again comes to visit, grab your list and remind him that there is another way to look at the world and your life!

Attitude of Gratitude

At the end of my workshops, I ask delegates what they have gained from the day and link back to what they wanted when they arrived. On this particular day, a delegate had said that she was looking for direction—a new start in life: "I want to know where I am going and how I can get there." When the check in was asked at the end, she simply laughed, "I find it really funny that I wanted all of that at the start, and I now realise that I already have what I want. It has taken coming here to realise it!"

So much energy is spent searching for something else that you think will make you feel better, and you neglect to look around you and give gratitude for what you already do have: health, family, friends, clothes, a home, food, etc.

As Claire put it, "We take so many things for granted, and then we fail to realise how blessed we are."

Take 5 minutes each day—best in the morning—and practise an attitude of gratitude, noticing what you have.

I remember one day, I rushed to park for a meeting that I was late for, due to traffic. My parking space was a 5-minute walk from the meeting, and it was raining. I heard myself say, "...and how on Earth can I be grateful for that?" Well, I was grateful that I had a car to get me there, healthy legs and water proof shoes to make the walk, and an umbrella to keep me dry.

You may have to look hard to find what you have to be grateful for sometimes, but believe me, when you start looking, you will realise that there really is so much to be grateful for—every day!

Trusting Your Instincts

I find it fascinating how often clients tell me that when they listen to their instincts (however that shows for them), things change.

Much of Wendy's story is about her following her instincts—from realising coaching could move her forward to the big decision of moving to Australia, to expos she went to and even to getting their visas. Your instincts can be very subtle. Everyone has them; you just may have lost trust as to where they are or how to recognise them!

Some people go on their gut instinct—a feeling or sensation that they have that indicates whether to go for something or not, which they feel (yep, you guessed it) in their gut! For others, it may be that something just did or didn't look or sound right. There is no correct way to follow your instincts; only you will know what they are for you.

This is something that you have to practise and nurture. It is always there and always happening, but are you hearing, seeing or feeling it? Think about when you were looking for a house (or car, partner or job). Did you go for the look or feel of it? Or was there something else inside that you could hear that supported you in making that choice?

Instincts are not easy to trust because they happen first and are usually very subtle. A split second later, the mind will come in with its two cents' worth of ideas. As you listen to your mind, guess who gets the most attention and therefore the most trust? If you want to listen, feel and see your instincts and trust what they have to say, then you need to sit quietly and notice the response that comes in before the chatter in your head. This does take time, so have patience and allow yourself to go through the learning process, which means give yourself permission to make mistakes, learn from them, and grow!

The Home stretch

Breathe.

On reflection what did you gain from these exercises?

What can ONE you take away and put into immediate practice?

What do you need in order to help support you with this?

Remember that it is just a process of learning, no right or wrong answers.

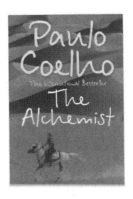

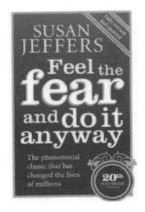

Recommended Books

<u>*Recommended Films*</u>

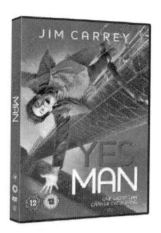

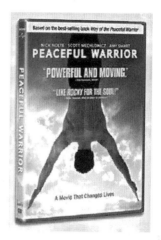

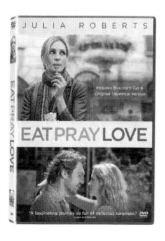

As I am completing this book I realised that all these films are all based on real life events. They haven't been made up or constructed for entertainment purposes. They show how many people change their lives by taking responsibility, keeping going, taking opportunities.

If they can, you can too :-)

Finally...

I trust that you have found these stories inspiring. Hopefully giving you the belief that if we can you sure can too! I want to thank Claire, Helen, Wendy, Sarah, and Fiona for taking the time to share their journeys and insights. I know that behind each one of them is the intention to help and inspire someone else. I am grateful to them for supporting this project so that I could offer you the tools and techniques that have made the biggest differences for them. As I think you may gather, there are more, but use the breakdown of these exercises, choose one and commit to doing that for 7 days. By doing so, you WILL see a difference in your life. It probably won't happen overnight, but stick with it. Be patient, and you will see the magic!

If you would like to stay in touch, then please join us on our www.facebook.com/TheConfidenceGarden

I would like to join the ladies in this book in wishing you blessings on your journey from wherever you are.

All you need to do is *take control*, take it *one step at a time,* and *believe in yourself.* Your life depends on it!

About Jules

"When you get stuck in a rut, don't make it home."

It took leaving a ten year career to realise just how low my self belief and self confidence was. I could have stayed there and wallowed, I very nearly did. The moment I realised that *I* had the power to do things differently though, everything changed. Since then I have studied and trained in a variety of techniques and methodologies with teachers from around the world.

Coaching is about holding up a mirror for clients. Reflecting perspectives, possibilities and opportunities, that they may well not see. Through each coaching conversation, insights create a new experience of life, and for many the chance to access their inner wisdom. This philosophy isn't something that just stays within working hours. For me this is an exciting way of living. Exploring each day for possibilities and opportunities.

I may still get nervous when I see these opportunities, but I don't let the nerves decide whether I take it or not. That means I have said *yes* to many things in the past decade or so that I never believed I would or could do; hiking to Machu Piccu, cycling in Cambodia, abseiling the Humber bridge, sky diving from 15,000 feet or appearing *in front* of the camera on BBC Breakfast TV after spending years back stage.

Working with Jules

1:1 & Group Coaching

Jules' coaching is based in a number of methodologies. After years of training and working with clients, it now reaches beyond the purist coaching model to help you understand resilience, gain certainty in uncertain times and take confidence to a new authentic level, i.e. no more 'faking it'!

To explore the possibility of coaching with Jules please contact info@positive-belief.co.uk or you can visit www.juleswyman.com to download the full coaching brochure.

Online Confidence Programme

Imagine building a strong foundation of authentic confidence. What difference could that create in your life? That is precisely what the T.R.U.S.T. system online coaching programme offers. A 6 week programme, with lifetime access. Full of videos, audios, workbooks and interviews for you to build lasting confidence.

Head to www.juleswyman.com/trustsystem for more information and get started on creating lasting confidence today.

More Information

For more information on booking Jules to bring confidence to your events please contact:

info@positive-belief.co.uk

01904 270944

Acknowledgements.

I believe that people come into your life for a reason and I have been blessed with some wonderful people in the last few years that have supported me and this work in a number of ways.

Tiffany, Veronika and Tabitha, my soul sisters. Thank you for your guidance, challenges and inspiration. What would I have done without those Skype calls!

Ann, 'my pumpkin'. Your words of encouragement have meant so much coming from such a prolific writer and reader.

To all my family, especially my mum, you 'indulged' my randomness and have given me a freedom to explore the world, even when you aren't quite sure what I am up to next. Thank you for teaching me the basics of common sense and politeness.

22333776R00050

Made in the USA
Columbia, SC
31 July 2018